Military History Sources f(

The Anglo-Boer War 1899-1902

Phil Tomaselli

FEDERATION OF FAMILY HISTORY SOCIETIES - (PUBLICATIONS) LIMITED -

Published by
The Federation of Family History Societies (Publications) Ltd
Units 15-16 Chesham Industrial Centre
Oram Street, Bury
Lancashire BL9 6EN

ISBN: 1 86006 197 4

First published 2006

Printed and bound at The Alden Press
Osney Mead, Oxford OX2 0EF

Contents

On guard

SECTION 1

Overview

The South African War of 1899 to 1902 (popularly known as the Boer War) was the biggest conflict that the British Army took part in between Waterloo and the start of World War One. Over 400,000 British and Imperial troops fought a long, hard and dangerous war against the armies of the two Boer republics of the Orange Free State and Transvaal then, when the two republics were forced to surrender, against guerrilla forces (known as commandos) who refused to give in.

The origins of the war were complex and reached back to the early days of the 19th century when Britain occupied the Dutch colony in South Africa during the Napoleonic wars. The native Dutch colonists, Afrikaners or Boers, resented imposed authority and when Britain banned slavery, many trekked inland and set up the two independent republics.

Attempts by the British to incorporate them into a greater South Africa were rejected and resulted in the First Boer War of 1881 when, after a shock defeat, the British decided to leave them well alone. The discovery of gold and diamonds in South Africa in the 1870s and 1880s had caused great friction. With Britain annexing territories that the Boers thought should have been theirs and thousands of foreign workers (called Uitlanders), many of them British, flocking to prospect and work in the Republics.

Fearful of being 'swamped' by the outsiders, the Boers refused them the vote. The ill-conceived Jameson Raid in December 1895, when troops employed by the British South Africa Company tried, and failed, to stage a coup increased resentment. Thinking that another war was inevitable, the Boer Republics spent millions on weapons and, in October 1899, with talks stalled and the British planning to reinforce their army in South Africa, the Boers struck first.

Armed with the latest rifles, artillery and machine guns the Boers advanced into Natal and other British colonies. The British armies, which had spent the last 40 years fighting poorly armed native armies, had neither the weapons nor the tactics to face the highly mobile and well armed Afrikaners.

British soldiers were still tough and dedicated professionals and, though often badly punished, they held together and fell back. One army dug in at the railway junction of Ladysmith in Natal, another around the diamond mines at Kimberley while Baden Powell's small force did the same at Mafeking. Under siege by Boer armies, they held out and waited for reinforcements and relief.

The series of shock defeats galvanised the British government, who rushed in reinforcements. Australia, Canada and New Zealand also sent troops and volunteers poured in from all over the Empire. They learned new tactics of fire and movement: thousands of mounted troops, who could move and fight like the Boers, were recruited. Though casualties were often heavy, the sieges were raised, and the Boer armies were gradually pushed back into the Republics.

The great soldiers, Lords Roberts and Kitchener, came out to command the British armies. They advanced slowly, wearing

Lord Roberts (1832-1914), Commander in Chief of British Forces in South Africa during 1900. Universally known as 'Bobs' he was extremely popular with the troops.

down the much smaller Boer armies in a series of set piece battles, which their opponents were not so well equipped to fight. Though some of the more far-sighted Boer leaders, such as De Wet, urged that they should try mobile guerrilla tactics, the Boer leadership continued to try and fight a conventional war. In March 1900, Bloemfontein, capital of the Orange Free State, fell to Roberts. He renamed the country the Orange River Colony and pressed on into the Transvaal. On 31st May, Johannesburg surrendered and on 2nd June, Pretoria, capital of the Transvaal, fell.

The main army of the Orange Free State surrendered at the end of July. During August, September and October the combined British armies harried the remaining Boer field armies. President Kruger of the Transvaal fled to Europe.

On 25th October, Roberts proclaimed the annexation of the Transvaal, announced the war was "nearly over" and returned to England to receive an Earldom.

He left Kitchener behind to finish the mopping up operations. No one on the British side expected the war to last another 18 months, believing the remaining Boer forces would surrender and go home. Unfortunately the British had not reckoned with the brilliant and charismatic Boer leaders De Wet, De la Rey, Smuts and Botha who led much smaller forces in a series of guerrilla raids against the ponderous British supply trains and isolated garrisons. They even struck deep into Cape Colony and Natal where they hoped to kindle support amongst the Boers who lived there. Fortunately for the British they remained loyal to the Crown.

To wear down the Boer commandos the British began to build a network of blockhouses, linked by barbed wire fences, across the countryside, breaking up the territory in which the guerrillas operated. The British also took to burning Boer farms and crops and moving families, many of whom had been

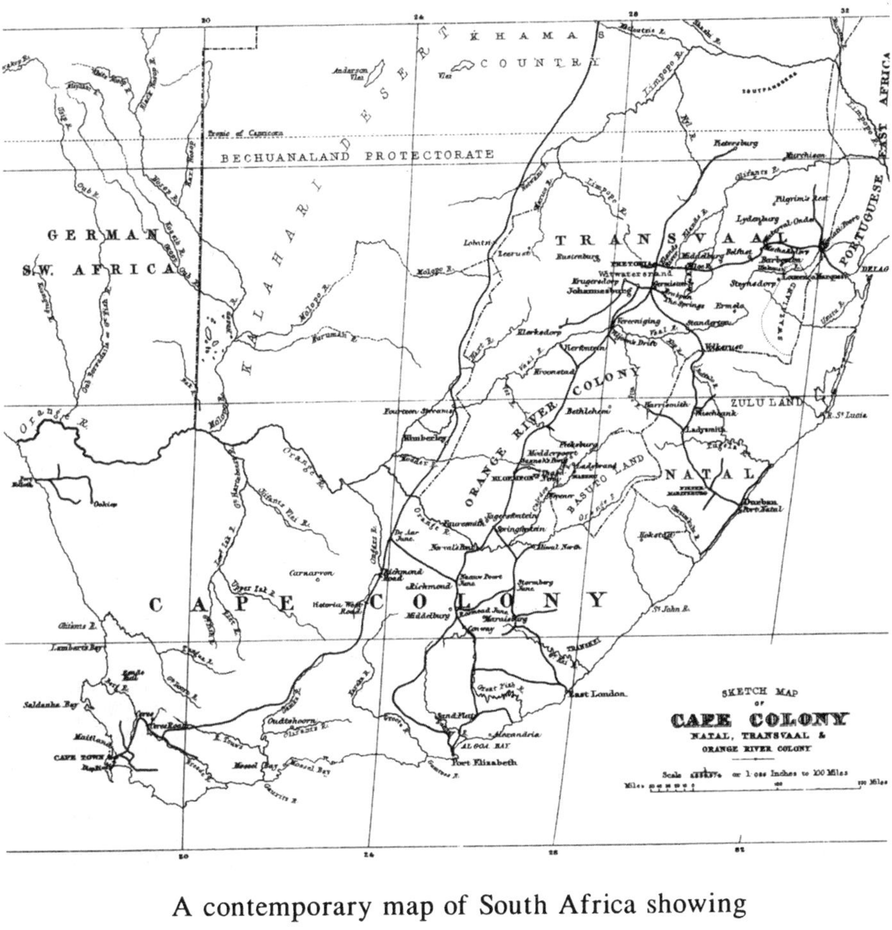

A contemporary map of South Africa showing the main transport routes.

secretly supplying the commandos with food and shelter, into concentration camps. Here epidemics of typhoid and dysentery soon took hold. Thousands of women and children became seriously ill and many died, leading to allegations of a deliberate policy of genocide.

Many black Africans, having originally been driven from their land by the Boers, began to move back on to the deserted farms and to attack the commandos. A Zulu force attacked and wiped out a commando that entered Zululand in 1902.

Faced with overwhelming odds, and more importantly, with the loss of the farms and families they had fought so long and hard for, the Boer commandos agreed that, though they had vowed to fight to 'the bitter end', the bitter end had now come. On 31st May 1902 they agreed to lay down their arms when they signed the Treaty of Vereeniging. The peace settlement brought to an end the Transvaal and the Orange Free State as Boer republics.

It had been a bitter, bloody and expensive war for both sides. The British and Commonwealth countries put some 447,435 men into the field and lost 42,000 to Boer weapons and disease. Of the 87,000 Boers who fought over 7,000 were killed, as well as between 18,000 and 28,000, mostly civilians, who died in the camps. The British army "expended" over 400,000 horses and mules; almost all the Boer farm cattle, sheep and horses were looted or killed. As part of the peace process the British government paid out over £5,000,000 in compensation. The ill feeling engendered between the British and Boers still simmers in some quarters today.

SECTION 2

Did My Ancestor Fight in the Boer War?

Almost every British army regiment sent troops to the Boer war though some individual battalions of each regiment (almost all had two battalions and some more) remained on garrison duty elsewhere in the Empire. However, they provided reinforcements to help their sister battalions where necessary.

John Stirling, *British Regiments in South Africa* (1903, reprinted by J B Hayward & Sons, 1994) gives details of the service of every British unit that took part in the campaign, based on the Commander in Chief's despatches.

To help out with what became an acute manpower shortage many of the reserve Militia battalions were embodied (called up). Some served in South Africa itself, others served on St Helena guarding prisoners of war and some were sent out to other colonies to act as garrisons to release regular troops for the war. Additional battalions were recruited in a major expansion of the army and additional short-term units, such as the Imperial Yeomanry and locally raised troops also served. It was an "unlucky" soldier who did not serve in the war if he wanted to.

The war marked the first occasion on which Canada dispatched troops to an overseas war. A total of 7,368 Canadians (and 12 Nursing Sisters) served in South Africa. Many thousands of Australians and New Zealanders volunteered and served in army units raised in the native countries. Many men also travelled, at their own expense, to volunteer for units being raised in South Africa. Information and copies of service records can be obtained from the relevant record offices in Australia, New Zealand and Canada (see 4 below).

In addition a large number of units, often with romantic or dashing names, were recruited in South Africa largely from British settlers.

Remember that in this period of Empire the idea of nationhood was still, to some extent, fluid. An Englishman living in the USA would have felt just as comfortable hopping over the border to enlist with a Canadian unit as he would returning to Britain. You may find an ancestor serving with a "colonial" unit, even though you had always regarded him as British.

Unless indicated all the records described in this Guide are to be found at The National Archives (TNA) (formerly the Public Record Office) at Kew. Most of the records described here have been microfilmed and are now available only in the Microfilm Reading Room. It is likely that over the next few years they will be digitised and made available online.

Records at TNA are arranged by department and then by type (known as series or classes). Individual volumes, files, maps or boxes of documents are referred to as pieces. Some tips about making the use of your time are in Appendix 2.

Driver William Robertson of the Imperial Volunteers.

Officers and troopers of the Angus Volunteers
who served in South Africa.

SECTION 3

Medals

Two campaign medals were awarded for Boer War Service, the Queen's South Africa Medal (QSA) and the King's South Africa Medal (KSA). Many families still have their ancestor's medals tucked away so these are a good place to start. An article about them appeared in the April 2005 issue of *Ancestors* Magazine.

The QSA was awarded to all who served in South Africa between 11 October 1899 and 31 May 1902. It has Queen Victoria's head on the front (obverse) and, on the back (reverse), Britannia holding the Union Flag in her left hand and a laurel wreath in her right. The words South Africa are around the top. The medal ribbon is orange with blue edge stripes and red edges. The medal could be awarded with a combination of "bars" or "clasps", each of which commemorates a particular battle or part of the campaign. These are important in trying to piece together an ancestor's service during the war.

Five clasps are for service within one of the colonies that made up South Africa at the time: Cape Colony, Natal, Rhodesia, Transvaal and Orange Free State. If a medal does not have one of these clasps, check that it is not a Queen's

Mediterranean Medal. This was awarded to the men, many of them volunteers or old soldiers, who filled gaps in battalions who sent drafts from Malta and Gibraltar to reinforce their sister battalions in South Africa.

In addition to the State clasps, other clasps were awarded for participation in some of the major battles and will tell you a lot about an individual's service. The bars include "Defence of Mafeking", "Defence of Kimberley", "Relief of Kimberley", "Laing's Neck" and "Tugela Heights". Once you know your ancestor took part in a particular battle, and the unit they served in, you can begin to look at reports, books, magazines and museums for more specific information.,

The KSA was awarded for service in 1901 and 1902. It has King Edward VII's head on the front with Britannia and the flag and wreath on the back. The medal ribbon is Green, White and Orange in equal vertical stripes. Only two bars were awarded: "South Africa 1901" and "South Africa 1902".

Each QSA and KSA will have, round the rim, the name, service number and unit that the ancestor served with, though for some of the more unusual units this may be hard to decipher. "FID" for example, is the Field Intelligence Department (mostly scouts), and "C. In C. BDYGD" is the Commander in Chief's Bodyguard, a specialist cavalry unit raised by Lord Roberts himself. It may take time to work out which particular unit your ancestor served with, but it is important to know.

Medal Rolls

Medal Rolls were compiled after the war by the units that took part and list all the men (and a few women, such as the nurses) who qualified for a medal as a result of their service.

The Medal Rolls for the Army are held in series WO 100, starting with WO 100/112 and running up to WO 100/383. The records are organised by unit, so that, for example, the Roll for 1st and 2nd Life Guards, Royal Horse Guards and 1st, 2nd and 3rd Dragoon Guards is in WO 100/112. It is comparatively easy to find the roll for a given unit by searching the TNA catalogue (www.nationalarchives.gov.uk/catalogue), looking for the unit name in WO 100. Paper indexes exist at Kew for those less keen on using computers.

Each roll is set out more or less alphabetically (though officers usually come first) and will give you your ancestor's rank and regimental number and tell you which campaign bars he was entitled to. The Medal Roll for the 2nd Battalion, Norfolk Regiment, for example, shows men awarded bars for Cape Colony, Orange Free State and Transvaal, as well as for the battles at Paaderberg and Johannesburg.

Every Victorian campaign included sailors and Royal Marines who often fought ashore as part of a Naval Brigade, and the Boer war was no exception. Heavy guns were manhandled off the ships, mounted on carriages and sent inland to support the army. The annual field gun race at the Royal Tournament commemorates the role the sailors and Marines played in moving their guns across country into action.

The Naval Medal Rolls are in ADM 171/52-54 and include sailors and Royal Marines. The Roll is by ship and then alphabetical, but as only a few ships took part it isn't too time consuming to find your ancestor even if you do not know which ship he served on. The Roll will not only tell you which ship he served with, but also his rank, which clasps he was entitled to, his Continuous Service Number (CSN) and to which ship the medal was sent. Please note that the bars to which an individual was entitled are indicated by numbers, but that there is a key at the start of the index which will tell you what each man's entitlement was. Rolls of honours for a

Reverse of Queen's and Kings South African Medals awarded for service during the war.

Obverse of Queen's and Kings South African Medals awarded for service during the war.

number of ships have been published TNA library has a selection of these.

Gallantry medals

Several awards were available for acts of gallantry, most notably the Victoria Cross (VC). In all, 78 VC's were awarded during the war. They are described at www.victoriacross.net/camp.asp. A brief account of the circumstances in which the medal was awarded (known as a citation) was published in the *London Gazette*. Uniquely, for the time, the Victoria Cross could be awarded to both officers and other ranks/ratings.

As well as the VC, the Distinguished Service Order (DSO) was awarded for bravery to junior officers in both services and in 1901 the Distinguished Service Cross (DSC) for Naval officers was created.

Other ranks were entitled to the Distinguished Conduct Medal (DCM). Recipients are listed in P E Abbott, *Recipients of the Distinguished Conduct Medal, 1855-1909* (J B Hayward and Son, 1975). TNA has a copy and you may find copies in other libraries and museums.

South African War Honours and Awards 1899-1902 (Arms & Armour Press 1971), is a reprint of an original book of 1902 compiled by the *Army & Navy Gazette* and lists all the gallantry and good conduct awards that had appeared in the *London Gazette* during the course of the war. There is a copy in TNA library.

Many men were "mentioned in despatches" for their heroism or meritorious conduct during the campaign. Their names were recorded in the despatches sent to London and later printed in the London Gazette. There is no other list and recipients (at this time) were not awarded a medal or other symbol to wear on their uniform notifying the award. Their details are published in *South African War Honours and*

Awards, 1899-1920: Officers and Men of the Army and Navy Mentioned in Despatches (Greenhill, 1987). TNA has a copy of this book.

Helping a wounded comrade.

Officers of the Angus Volunteers who served in South Africa.

SECTION 4

Service Records

Even if you do not have a medal, you might have been told that as ancestor served or have photographs, letters or some memorabilia that suggests that they did. Does what you have identify the man's unit? A badge might tell you which regiment he belonged to if you check it against a reference book at your local library. Pay books or other official correspondence should refer to which unit he served with. Letters might mention the name of his regiment, the names of his officers or tell you where he was serving at a given time. You can use the *Army List* to match his officers or location to a unit.

The National Archive (TNA) at Kew publishes a research guide *British Army: Useful Sources for Tracing Soldiers* which can be downloaded from their website.

The Army

Officers

Tracing officers is always easier than finding ordinary soldiers. There are two published lists for the period and both are available on the open shelves of the Microfilm Reading Room at Kew. Large regional libraries may have copies of the *Army Lists* or be able to obtain copies through Inter-Library Loan at a modest cost.

The official *Army List* was published quarterly by the War Office and will tell you which regiment your officer served in, and what his rank was. There is an index which will show you the page(s) he appears on. You can trace his previous promotions and his later career by looking at earlier and later editions. The list also contains a list of retirements, casualties and officers who have ceased to serve for other reasons (such as dismissal, cashiering and transportation for various military offences) but, though it gives the name and regiment, it rarely gives any more information.

Checking an edition from a couple of years after the war might tell you something about what your officer actually did during the fighting. There is a section, separate from the main listing, which gives officers' war services, telling you about which campaigns they served in and occasionally giving details of individual actions.

Many officers were separated from their regiments and sent to work in transport, intelligence and to be on the Staff which planned battles and organised the Brtish Army in South Africa. There are over 20 pages in the list showing to which units they were attached and where they were deployed.

Hart's Army List is an invaluable source of information on officers for most of the 19th century, though by the time of the Boer War the official War Office list carries much the same information. It is always worth checking as *Hart's* does occasionally contain additional material. Copies of *Hart's* are also on the shelves in the Microfilm Room at Kew.

Regiments kept records of officers' service and these can be found in WO 76, which is held on microfilm at TNA and are partially indexed. A card index can be found in the Microfilm Reading Room. These records are organised by regiment so you may need to check more than one volume if you cannot find your officer in the index. These records will give you basic information about the officer's enlistment, where he served and when, which actions he took part in and his family (if he married).

Many relatively junior officers continued to serve into the First World War or even beyond, so you may need to check later service records. Those for the First World War are at Kew in series WO 338, WO 339 and WO 374. It is easy to see whether there are documents for your man, because all the records are listed on the online catalogue.

If they continued to serve after 1922 their papers have not yet been released but many will feature in *Who's Who* and this will give you some idea of their service. You will need to contact the Army Records Office at Glasgow to request their papers (details at www.veteransagency.mod.uk).

Other ranks

Series WO 97 is probably the best place to start when looking for a Boer War soldier's service records if you know that he survived to receive a pension. This series contains enlistment and discharge papers for men who survived their army service and were discharged. The papers will show place and date of birth, age on enlistment, and a physical description. Discharge papers between 1900 and 1913 are between references WO 97/4232 and WO 97/6323. For this period they are collected alphabetically for the whole army. Some misfiled papers have been gathered together and are in alphabetic sequence between WO 97/6355 and WO 97/6383.

The records will tell when and where a man enlisted, provide a physical description, list promotions and next of kin, and where a man served and for how long. There should also be a note giving the reason for a man's discharge.

The Medal Roll for 2nd Battalion Norfolk Regiment shows that Private 4969, John Gooderham, was entitled to bars for his QSA Medal for Cape Colony, Orange Free State and Transvaal. His service record is in WO 97/4952, which indicates that he enlisted, age 18 years and 4 months at Norwich on 11 July 1898. He was born at Hempnall, Norfolk and was five feet seven and a half inches tall with a sallow complexion, brown hair and hazel eyes. He served 8 years with the colours (that is regular army), forfeited a good conduct badge (then had it restored), served in South Africa from 4 January 1901 to 10 February 1903 and again for 6 months in 1905/6. He married Lucy Sabina Rayson at Norwich Register Office on 2 November 1907, when still serving with the reserves, that is former soldiers who could be called up in time of national emergency.

Many men who saw action in the Boer War were either still serving, or rejoined the colours, at the start of the First World War so their papers would have been amalgamated with the World War I records.

Unfortunately about 60% of WW1 soldiers records were destroyed in the Blitz so if you cannot find anything in WO 97 try checking the Medal Cards which are, available online at www.documentsonline.nationalarchives.gov.uk or on microfiche at Kew. If your ancestor served abroad during the War, and was thus entitled to a medal, you can at least have a good idea that his papers had been amalgamated. TNA holds, on microfilm, the remaining papers (some of them only partial because of fire damage) of soldiers, and their website will tell you how to go about looking for these. There are several TNA research guides which can be downloaded from the Archive's website explaining how to go about tracing ancestors who fought in the First World War.

Irregular soldiers

In addition to the regular and militia troops who served during the war there were many thousands more who enlisted with locally recruited garrisons, irregular cavalry or units specially recruited in Britain and the colonies for war service.

The Imperial Yeomanry

It was recognised early in the war that the army faced a severe shortage of mounted infantry so the War Office raised, through the existing Yeomanry cavalry organisation, a force that eventually totalled some 40,000 officers and men for service in South Africa.

Recruits had to be between the ages of 20 and 35, of good character, who could ride and shoot. Men were to provide their own horse, clothing and saddle with the government providing guns, ammunition and equipment.

The first group of volunteers included many from the upper strata of society. The 13th Battalion had a company of Irish huntsmen which included the Earl of Longford and Viscount Ennismore, and the Ulster Protestant companies included the Earl of Leitrim, Sir John Power and the future Lord Craigavon. When a second contingent was recruited in early 1901 recruits tended to be working rather than middle class, motivated less by patriotism than by the promise of five shillings a day pay. A third recruiting drive in late 1901 produced another 10,000 men who arrived in the closing days of the war and who stayed in South Africa until 1903 to assist the process of pacification.

Records for the Imperial Yeomanry are held at the National Archive in Kew. Short Service attestation papers are in WO 128/34, arranged by service number, and these will tell you where the man was recruited, address, next of kin and in which unit and which parts of South Africa he served. If the man went on to serve as a Regular his papers may be in WO 97.

Archie Bone, son of an East India Merchant, joined up on 12 February 1900 at Buckingham. He served in South Africa between March 1900 and July 1901 in the 56th Company of the 15th Battalion. His medal entitlement shows that he served in Cape Colony, the Orange Free State and Transvaal and, though he came out of the Yeomanry before the end of hostilities, he obviously had acquired a taste for army life as he soon joined the Indian Army as an officer.

Officers' records for the Yeomanry do not seem to have survived. One tip is to check records for the First World War as many officers and men re-enlisted and some papers from the Boer War may be with their records.

There are further rolls of Yeomanry Officers, Non-Commissioned Officers and men, organised by unit, in WO 108/93-95, and you may find additional details here.

South Africa Medals entitlements are listed in WO 100/120-130 and WO 100/356-357. Awards of the Imperial Yeomanry Long Service and Good Conduct Medals were announced in Army Orders: details are now in WO 123.

If you think that you might have an ancestor amongst the Imperial Yeomanry the best place to start is by visiting http://hometown.aol.co.uk/kevinasplin/home.html, where Kevin Asplin has diligently recorded the names of all 40,000 Imperial Yeomen and associated units. He has also produced a book *Roll of the Imperial Yeomanry, Scottish Horse and Lovat Scouts 1899-1902*, which is available from DP&G Publishing, PO Box 186, Doncaster DN4 0HN. Copies are available at TNA and the Family Records Centre in Islington.

An article about the Imperial Yeomanry appeared in *Family History Monthly* no 104 (May 2004).

Irregular units

In addition to the Imperial Yeomanry there were a large number of irregular cavalry and a few infantry units. They were generally recruited in South Africa itself, but many thousands of men travelled to fight from all over the world. Units had such diverse names as The Commander in Chief's Bodyguard, The Umvoti Rifles, The Cape Town Highlanders and The Transkei Mounted Rifles. A full list, together with brief histories of individual units are given in John Stirling, *The Colonials in South Africa, 1899-1902: being the services of the various irregular corps raised in South Africa and the contingents from Australia, Canada, New Zealand, India and Ceylon together with details of those mentioned in despatches with related honours and awards* (J. B. Hayward and Son, 1990). TNA Library has a copy.

Service was generally for six months, at which time a man was free to leave, but many chose to re-enlist with another unit which was offering a higher recruitment bounty. To try to prevent men switching units it was announced that the bounty would be paid only to men who hadn't served before. This resulted in a lot of men re-enlisting under variants of their name, which can cause problems for researchers trying to build up a coherent picture of an individual's service.

As an example, The Commander-in-Chief's Bodyguard Medal Roll for the QSA Medal has a Sgt D Frame (Number 22295). The Nominal Roll gives him as Daniel. It also gives previous service for D Frame with Cape Town Highlanders (1151), South Africa Light Horse (407) and Kitchener's Horse (4070).

The records for Cape Town Highlanders are sparse and make no references to anyone named Frame. The Record of Service for the South Africa Light Horse lists David Frame, age 24, occupation engineer, next of kin Mrs H Frame, 17

Budhill Avenue, Shettleston, near Glasgow. Record of Service for D Frame, 4070 Kitchener's Horse, doesn't provide a next of kin but says he is going to New Zealand on discharge and their nominal roll gives him as David Ewart Frame: trade electrician.

There is also a mysterious David Ewart Frame who served with the Scottish Horse, albeit briefly. He is definitely the same man as South Africa Light Horse 407, as his next of kin is Mrs Hanna Frame, Budhill Terrace, Shettleston, Glasgow. He was kicked out for insubordination.

What we appear to have is one man jumping from unit to unit on completion of service (for one reason or another) and going where the bounty is highest. He may have called himself David in some units in an attempt to muddy the waters. It's also possible that it was the War Office who managed to muddle the records of two separate men. There is a certain amount of overlap, but on the other hand some records flatly contradict themselves.

Enrolment forms for locally raised units are in WO 126 and there are muster rolls (lists of which men were in which unit) in WO 127. The Medal Rolls are in WO 100, arranged by unit. Kevin Asplin's website http://hometown.aol.co.uk/KevinAsplin/home.html has nominal rolls for a few irregular units.

The records of the South African Constabulary, between 1900 and 1908, (which recruited many former British soldiers) and the Rand Rifles are held by the National Archives Repository, Private Bag X236, Pretoria, 0001, South Africa. The location of records for a few other South African-recruited units can be found at www.militarymuseum.co.za/main.htm.

The Royal Navy and Royal Marines

Navy Officers

The Admiralty published the *Navy List* on a quarterly basis but, like the *Army List* is often thin on the kind of information that a family historian might be interested in. You can trace an officer's promotions by looking through a run of the List and it will tell you when he was promoted to his current rank. The List will also tell you on which ship the officer was serving, give a list of his fellow officers and some details of the ship itself, as well as the Station (i.e., where it was serving). Because there is an index of names it is possible to trace an officer's movements from ship to ship throughout his career.

As well as the *Navy List* the Admiralty kept a *Service Register* which detailed an officer's career as it progressed. These are in series ADM 196. The records have been indexed and the results are on cards held in the Microfilm Reading Room at Kew. The documents were originally large ledgers and, for an officer who served for a long time, the references can be difficult to follow. When the Admiralty clerks ran out of space they'd often cram information into a space on an adjacent page or continue on a page some distance away. Watch out for this, and beware of someone else's information being crammed into what appears to be the record for your officer.

For Royal Marine officers from 1893 to 1925 there are detailed service records in ADM 196/58-65, 83 and 97-112.

Many Royal Navy and Royal Marine officer service records are summarised briefly in *The Naval Who's Who,* which was published in 1917, and includes both serving and retired officers. It was republished by J B Hayward and Son in 1981 and a copy is held by TNA Library.

More information about using these records can be found in a TNA Research Guide: *Royal Navy: Officers' Service Records*.

Other ranks: Sailors and Marines

Once you have obtained the Continuous Service Number (CSN) from the Naval Medal Roll or from the medal itself, you can trace an individual's service record. These are held in series ADM 188 and there is an index, which will show you which reel of microfilm holds the record you are looking for. Robert John Bean (CSN 191339) served on HMS *Barracouta* during the war and went ashore to fight. His service record is in ADM 188/327 and shows that he was born 16 June 1881 at Lydd in Kent. His trade on enlistment was 'Labourer' and he enlisted for 10 years. He was 18 years old when he joined in June 1899 but a careful reading of the record shows that he in fact enlisted underage, in December 1896. When he enlisted he was just over 5 feet tall but by 1899 he was over 5 feet 2 inches, so naval service must have agreed with him. The ships he served on are given, as well as two periods of seven days in the cells. He seems to have deserted in 1906 but volunteered again at the start of the First World War. He was given free passage to Canada, where he was discharged in 1915.

More information about using these records can be found in a TNA Research Guide: *Royal Navy: Ratings' Service Records 1667-1923*. The records themselves are available online at www.nationalarchives.gov.uk/documentsonline.

For Royal Marine Warrant Officers there are only three volumes of Service Records covering 1873-1920 in ADM 196/34 and 35, ADM 196/67 and ADM 196/102.

Records of Royal Marine other ranks are in series ADM 159, arranged by Division and Service Number. To find the service number use ADM 313/27-109.

TNA has several research guides on Royal Marine records.

A few papers relating to naval personnel are held at the Fleet Air Arm Museum at Yeovilton. These consist of ratings' enlistment papers for Ships' Police and Sick Berth Attendants recruited between 1888 and 1919 and these include some Boer War servicemen. A rating's enlistment papers are supposed to contain only basic personal information such as next of kin, address, brief physical description and where enlisted. It is obvious, however, that much other material has been bound with them, including disciplinary papers, next of kin details and some information about education.

Colonial Units

Small numbers of troops from the six colonies in Australia (which only became a unified country on 1 January 1901), Canada and New Zealand also served in South Africa. Although at the time this was seen as being an example of the Empire united behind a common cause, subsequent historians have detected stirrings of nationalist feeling, particularly with regard to the court martial of the Australian officer Harry 'Breaker' Morant.

John Stirling, *The Colonials in South Africa 1899-1902* (1907, reprinted by J B Hayward & Son, 1990) gives details of the service of every Colonial unit that took part in the campaign, including the locally based irregulars and Australian, Canadian and New Zealand troops, based on the Commander in Chief's despatches.

The records are largely available online.

Australia

Records are largely held either by the National Archives of Australia or the Australian War Memorial and there are links to online databases to nominal and casualty rolls for all Australian troops who were in South Africa at:

www.awm.gov.au/research/infosheets/south_africa.asp.

www.naa.gov.au/the_collection/family_history/armed_services.html#boer_war

will take you to the section of the Australian National Archive which describes their holdings of soldiers' records.

Another excellent website devoted to the war is at http://users.westconnect.com.au/~ianmac/boermain.html.

Canada

A summary of Canadian involvement in the War is at www.civilization.ca/cwm/disp/dis008_e.html. Lists of men who served with the Canadian forces including casualties can be found at www.afhs.ab.ca/publications/armstrong/boer. A roll of honour for Canadians who lost their lives in South Africa is at www.vac-acc.gc.ca/general/sub.cfm?source=collections/books/safrica.

Service records are online at the Library and National Archives of Canada (www.collectionscanada.ca) in Ottawa. There is a search facility to allow you to find an ancestor even if you are not sure of all his (or her) details.

The British Isles Family History Society of Greater Ottawa has indexed the records and published the results as *Index to Canadian Service Records of the South African War (1899-1902) held at the National Archives of Canada* (Ottawa, 1999). www.collectionscanada.ca/military/h13-1003-e.html has a brief introduction to the part played by the Canadians during the war, and includes databases to service files, medal registers and land grant applications made by troops who subsequently returned to Canada.

New Zealand

Links to records relating to New Zealanders who served in South Africa can be found at www.nzhistory.net.nz/Gallery/SAW/index.html. They include lists of men who embarked for South Africa and a roll of honour for those who did not return.

Service records for the Boer War are with Archives New Zealand in Wellington. Details can be found at www.archives.govt.nz/doingresearch/nzdfpersonnelfiles.html.

On patrol

A memorial to the dead of the Boer War in Trinity Cemetery, Aberdeen.

SECTION 5

Other Sources

The Boers

Should your ancestor have been on the Boer side, there is no existing comprehensive list of participants. However, if he applied for the Dekoratie voor Trouwe Dienst, which was issued eighteen years after the end of hostilities, his name, rank and commando will appear on *Die Medeljerol: Dekoratie voor Trouwe Dienst Anglo-Boeroorlog*, *die Zuid Afrikaansche Republiek* or *Oranje Vrijstaat Oorlogsmedalje: Lint voor verwonding opgedaan gedurende die Anglo-Boereoorlog*. If he was a Boer prisoner of war, try the two volumes of *Boer Forces POW Roll: Boer War 1899-1902*. The War Museum of the Boer Republics may be a good place to seek further information. It has details of Boer prisoners of war and pensioners organisations: Anglo-Boer War Museum, PO Box 34061, Faunasig, South Africa 9325, www.anglo-boer.co.za.

A selection of claims made by Boer farmers and their families for damage caused during the war are to be found in series WO 148. There is no nominal index, so you will need to know where your ancestors were living when they made their claim.

Casualty records

Some 42,000 died during the War, most to disease rather than enemy action. A complete list of men who died or who wounded in action is in WO 108/360 and has been published as Frank and Andrea Cook, *South Africa Field Force Casualty List, 1899-*1902 (London, 1972). This is arranged by unit rather than by name, so it may be easier to use Alexander M Palmer's *The Boer War Casualty Roll, 1899-1902: An Alphabetical Listing* (Military Minded, 1999), which lists casualties alphabetically giving such details as the unit they were with, what type of casualty they were (killed, wounded, captured, died of wounds), place and date they became a casualty.

For men who served in Natal check *The South African War Casualty Roll: The 'Natal Field Force' 20th Oct. 1899 - 26th October 1900*. Copies of all these books are available at Kew.

Other lists of casualties are in WO 108/89-91, 338 and WO 25. Naval losses are recorded in ADM 116/529. A list of soldiers from the colonies buried in Cape Province is DO 119/1479.

Short biographies of officers who lost their lives can be found in Mildred G. Dooner's *The "Last Post": being a Roll of all Officers (Naval, Military or Colonial) who gave their lives for their Queen, King and country in the South African War, 1899-1902* (Simpkins, 1903, reprinted J B Hayward and Son, 1980). TNA Library has a copy.

The South African Heritage Resources Agency has a computerised database for all those who died in military conflicts on South African soil, including the Anglo-Boer War, which will tell you where a man is buried. Contact details: SAHRA, PO Box 8000, 2771 Cape Town, South Africa, email: dsibayl@sahra.org.za.

The Victorian Military Society is supporting a project to list all the surviving war memorials from the Boer War. More details can be found at www.casus-belli.co.uk/abwmp. There is already a list of nearly 1600 (with some inscriptions) on the United Kingdom National Inventory of War Memorials (www.ukniwm.org.uk).

Operational records

Individual units didn't keep war diaries during the Boer War (in fact they were introduced in 1907 as a result of the reforms that resulted from the War). This can make it difficult to find out what an individual unit was doing, but some information can be gained from the Staff Diaries in WO 32, which record troop movements and actions for their particular area, and from reports in WO 108, the Commander in Chief's papers. Diaries for December 1899 and January 1900 are in WO 32/7868 and 7876-7877. Those for the Natal Campaign for May and December 1900 are in WO 32/7901, 7951.

The best place to start may be the printed regimental histories, which describe (often in great detail) what individual units did. TNA Library has a reasonable collection and you can often find them in reference libraries and of course at regimental museums (see below).

If your ancestor had a clasp for "Ladysmith" or "Relief of Ladysmith" you can use the TNA website search facility to look for all references to Ladysmith during the period 1899 to 1902. (You can of course also do a similar search for other actions, such as Mafeking).

In the War Office papers (WO) the catalogue reveals 31 references, some to gallantry awards, some to the type of artillery used but most to operations around the town. Some even include reports written by quite junior officers about the fighting.

Captain Wilcox, of the Gloucestershire Regiment, wrote a report of one action from his hospital bed on 29 October 1899:

"All went well till we came to Hyde's Farm at the foot of the hill at about 1.30am. Here the mules were stampeded by a party of 3 or 4 Boers. All the guns, much small arms and Maxim ammunition was lost."

Captain Wilcox was not happy with the state of the defences he'd been ordered to man. "The advanced posts were too small and not enough under cover" and "the positions were too scattered". Fighting from behind a circle of rocks, Wilcox's "E" and "H" companies soon began to take casualties and Wilcox himself was shot through the arm. His men were ordered to link up with another company behind a stone wall.

For some hours, they held out until it was noticed that the Boers were working their way around their flank. "The next place of shelter was fully 200 yards back and the space between fully exposed to a fire that became hotter and more effective every second. I retired with the last few men on the left and was shot again through the shoulder."

The positions had not been thought out and "in my opinion the position was too large for the number of men and the loss of the guns in the morning was most unhappy. There was a little moonlight when we reached the hill top but the fire that began at daylight interfered with making proper dispositions." (WO 32/7861).

The Staff Diaries in WO 32 not only contain the diaries themselves but also reports on the health of troops, railway movements, arrivals at ports (giving names of officers and nurses) and handwritten notes made at the time. Do not expect to find a man named (unless he was an officer or awarded a gallantry medal) but you can build up quite a detailed picture of conditions from these diaries.

Another source is the South African War Papers in series WO 108, which consists chiefly of the correspondence of the Commander in Chief, South Africa (Lord Roberts) with reports and returns received by him from unit commanders. There are also some nice photographs of blockhouses to be found here. Similar papers are with Lord Roberts' personal papers in WO 105.

Also useful is the material in the War Office general correspondence (WO 32/7844-9119). Some intelligence reports, including reconnaissance reports, are in WO 33/152-198.

TNA also has several collections of private papers. Material from earlier in the war with the Buller Papers (WO 132). Several other commanders have collections of papers at TNA, including Maj Gen Sir John C. Ardagh (PRO 30/40), Col R.B. Colvin (WO 136), Lord Kitchener (PRO 30/57), and Brig Gen Sir H. Osborne Mance (PRO 30/66). Material in these classes tends to consist of dry official papers rather than more interesting personal letters or diaries.

There are also maps and plans of operations, most of which are to be found in series WO 78.

Letters home

Many officers, and some soldiers, wrote home regularly and the appropriate regimental museum or National Army Museum may have these. It can be difficult to trace individual correspondents, but two online resources may provide leads: Access to Archives (www.nationalarchives.gov.uk/a2a) and the National Register of Archives (www.nra.nationalarchives.gov.uk).

Newspapers

Newspaper coverage of the war was extensive and there was much competition amongst the press to report details: (so enthusiastic were they that the War Office pointed out gently to the editors that they were giving away valuable information to the enemy). Famous war correspondents were sent out and reported by telegraph to London. The most famous of these was Winston Churchill who went out to cover the war for *The Morning Post* at a salary of £250 per month. Shortly after his arrival, Boers ambushed the armoured train he was travelling on. Churchill helped to uncouple the engine and get it away but, along with fifty or so soldiers, he was taken prisoner and sent to a camp at Pretoria. After a short period of imprisonment he managed to escape and, helped by a British mine manager, escaped to Portuguese East Africa and then returned to England.

Local newspapers ran features on local men and units and organised charitable appeals to help the troops. Details of casualties are frequently reported, as well as of actions that the men took part in, usually derived from letters sent home to loved ones.

Your local studies library will usually hold copies of the local papers and of *The Times* for the period. If you want more information from this kind of source you can try the British Library's depository of newspapers and magazines at Colindale. There's an online database to the holdings at www.bl.uk/collections/newspapers.html.

TNA has a complete set of *The Times* on microfilm. In addition there is access to the Times Digital Archives through the computer terminals in the public areas at Kew: the whole of the newspaper can be searched by name or subject and you can read the newspaper on screen.

Shipping lists

Lists of ships going to South Africa were extracted from the *The Times and Cape Times* Shipping Lists, for the period July 1899 to December 1902, and provides details of the movement of troops in and out of the country and contains many references to individuals – mostly officers. It can found online at http://hometown.aol.co.uk/heatherasplin/home2.html.

Passenger lists for commercial liners (not troopships) are in BT 27 (outward bound) and BT 26 (inward bound). They may list individual officers and other ranks. Unless you know the exact name of the ship and time and place of departure/arrival it can be difficult to find individual documents. However there is an ongoing project to index inward passenger lists which should be complete by mid-2006 and another commercial one, to index and make the outward passenger lists available online by the end of 2007.

The Durban Archives Repository has passenger lists for all ships which arrived in Natal during the War: Durban Archives Repository, Private Bag X22, Greyville, South Africa 4023.

Women

A number of women served in South Africa, generally as nurses. No service records survive, but they are listed in the Royal Army Medical Corps medal rolls (WO 100/229, 353) and some information about the award of pensions is in WO 23/181. A few women were awarded the Royal Red Cross Medal for bravery or exceptional duty: rolls are in WO 145.

More information can be found in Anne Summers. *Angels and Citizens. British Women as Military Nurses 1854-1914* (Routledge and Kegan Paul, 1988) and especially Sheila Gray's *The South African War, 1899-1902: Service Records of British and Colonial Women. A Record of the Service in South Africa of Military and Civilian Nurses, Laywomen and Civilians* (Sheila Gray, 1993), which contains details of 1700 of the 2000 or so nurses who were in the theatre of operations. TNA library has copies of both books.

Museums

The National Army Museum tells the story of British land forces from the 15th Century to the present day. Although the Museum is an excellent place to find out about the general history of the Army they hold few official records, and are unlikely to be able to provide information on individual soldiers. However they do have a major archive and library with considerable holdings about the Boer War, so if you want to research a particular battle in more detail this is one of the places to visit. Indexes to some holdings are now on the Access to Archives website www.nationalarchives.gov.uk/a2a.

National Army Museum
Royal Hospital Road
London SW3 4HT
Tel. 020 7730 0717
www.national-army-museum.ac.uk

Regiments which took part in the war are justly proud of the part they played and usually feature it prominently in their museums. They often also hold material relating to their part in the war, ranging from copies of official documents to letters and reminiscences donated later by participants or their descendants. Regimental museums, addresses, opening hours are given in Terence and Shirley Wise, *A Guide to Military Museums and Other Places of Military Interest* (10th edition, Terence Wise, 2001). Similar information can be found on the web at www.armymuseums.org.uk.

Please remember that many museums have only a small staff and may take time to respond to queries and that a donation is often expected, or should be offered as a matter of courtesy, to help defray expenses..

The South African National Museum of Military History has many records relating to the South African forces as well as displays of artefacts and weapons. Its address is PO Box 52 090, Saxonwold 2132, www. militarymuseum.co.za. The website contains a useful page on researching ancestors who fought in South African forces.

APPENDIX 1

Books

Hundreds of books have been written about the war, both at the time and subsequently.

Thomas Pakenham, *The Boer War* (Weidenfeld and Nicholson, 1979) remains the best introduction. An illustrated and abridged edition was published in 1993.

Michael Carver, *The National Army Museum Book of the Boer War* (Sidgwick and Jackson, 1999) is another useful introduction.

There are numerous general books for the family historian on military and naval records. A valuable guide is Steve Dymond, *Researching British Military Medals* (Crowood Press, 1999) which, though primarily aimed at medal collectors, gives clear and concise explanations of the other records you can use to research a man's whole career.

Simon Fowler and William Spencer, *Army Records for Family Historians* (2nd edition, PRO, 1998) gives a concise description of the various records and shows lots of examples. It is rather dated, however, and readers might wish to use Simon Fowler, *Tracing Army Ancestors* (Pen and Sword, 2006) which covers much the same ground. Records of the militia and volunteers of the period are described in William Spencer, *Records of the Militia and Volunteer Forces, 1757-1945* (Public Record Office, 1997),

Bruno Pappalardo, *Tracing Your Naval Ancestors* (TNA, 2002) provides more details about naval records.

Cavalry charge

APPENDIX 2

Visiting The National Archives

The sheer amount of information available at the National Archives (TNA) can be daunting even for the experienced researcher and can overwhelm a first time visitor. Before visiting, take time to look at their website which has all the basic information you will need about getting there and how to register as a Reader (at no cost). There are excellent leaflets (research guides) which can be downloaded on various aspects of Military and Family history to help you in advance of your visit. Try using their online catalogue to look up documents that might be of interest (including some of the ones mentioned here) by browsing the categories (ADM for Admiralty and WO for War Office) until you come to references that look promising. You can also try the "Search" facility, which allows you to look for key words in document descriptions, but you may need to type in Transvaal or Natal, rather than South Africa, to find the documents, so you may need to use your imagination and a little patience to track down what you want.

It helps if you make yourself familiar with the TNA website before you visit (www.nationalarchives.gov.uk), which has a search engine to the 9.5m records held by the Archive and an extensive range of leaflets (Research Guides) which simply describe how to use many of the records in the Archives. There are also pages devoted to opening hours and if you can not visit TNA to do your own research there are lists of professional researchers who do the work for you for a fee.

Do not expect to find everything on one day. Be prepared to have to go back for more information. Obviously, the more work you are able to do beforehand in terms of looking at the catalogue and sorting out what it is you're looking for, the better and more productive your day will be.

On the Veld